Stand-up Comedy

by Cathy West

Ransom

StarStruck

Stand-up Comedy
by Cathy West

Illustrated by Georgina Fearns

Published by Ransom Publishing Ltd.
Radley House, 8 St. Cross Road, Winchester, Hants. SO23 9HX
www.ransom.co.uk

ISBN   978 184167 085 0

First published in 2014

Stand-up Comedy

Contents

All About
Stand-up
Comedy

What is stand-up comedy?

In stand-up comedy a person performs in front of a live audience.

The performer is called a comic, or comedian.

In stand-up comedy the comic *talks* to the audience.

So these are not stand-up comedy:

- 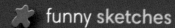 mime
- 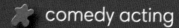 funny sketches
-  comedy acting
- slapstick.

Some comics just tell jokes.
Some comics tell funny stories.

Many comics tell stories about
what has happened to them.
(Most of it isn't true!)

Some comics use props, or
they mix comedy with magic
tricks or music.

Bill Bailey is an English stand-up
comedian. He is also a good musician.

His shows mix stand-up comedy with
music.

Where can you see stand-up comedy?

You can see stand-up comedy in **comedy clubs** or **theatres**.

At a comedy club you can see four or five acts in one show. Each comic has about twenty minutes on stage.

There is always a **headline** act. The headline act is the best-known comic. They always go on last.

Comic **Shappi Khorsandi** (from Iran) is often the headline act at comedy clubs.

Some of the biggest stand-up comics have their own TV shows.

You can also see stand-up comedy acts at comedy festivals.

The most famous comedy festivals are:

- Edinburgh Festival Fringe, Scotland, UK
- Melbourne International Comedy Festival, Australia
- Just for Laughs, Montreal, Canada.

John Bishop performing at the Edinburgh Festival Fringe.

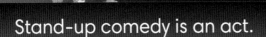

Stand-up comedy is an act.

- Some stand-up comics are happy and jolly in their act.

- Some are grumpy and miserable.

- Some pretend to be other people.

The Australian comic **Barry Humphries** *is* **Dame Edna Everage.**

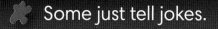 Some just tell jokes.

Some tell stories about their life.

Some are crazy.

Some make it up as they go along. This is called **improv**. Improv is very **risky**.

What if you have no ideas?

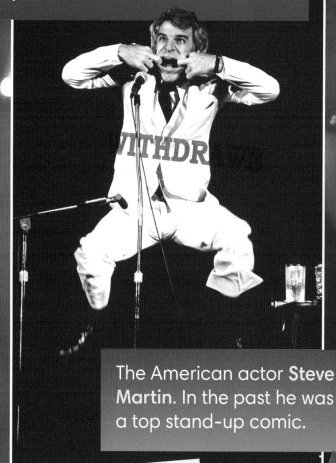

The American actor **Steve Martin**. In the past he was a top stand-up comic.

KK484712

11

A career in stand-up comedy

So you want to be a stand-up comic?

You need to be funny. This is very important!

You need to be good at timing. You must make the audience like you.

Stand-up comedy is hard. You must make people laugh.

If people don't laugh, it can get very bad!

Sometimes you will get hecklers. These are people in the audience who shout out at you.

Many stand-up comics do other things as well.

- They play music.

- They act.

- They write books or TV shows.

- Some even write jokes for other stand-up comics.

13

Getting started in stand-up comedy

Some comedy clubs have an **open mike** night.

This is when people from the **audience** can have five minutes on the stage to do some stand-up comedy.

You don't get paid for this. But it is a great way to get **experience**.

On an open mike night you can learn how to do stand-up in front of an audience.

If you are a good stand-up comic, you will get known. People will come to see you.

Then maybe you can start to do some **performances** for money.

How do I stay funny?

So, now you are a stand-up comic.

Remember: you will need to change your act often.

People don't want to see you doing the same old stuff each time!

All stand-up comics need to change their act.

But it can be hard to think of new jokes and new, funny stories.

If you are busy doing performances, maybe you don't have time to write new material.

Many stand-up comics pay other people to write new material for them.

Many stand-up comics get paid to write new material for other comics!

There is one thing you should never do:

Never steal jokes from other comics!

Chapter One
School joker

Jess Terr was the school joker. She loved to make people laugh with her funny stories.

But her teachers didn't see the funny side.

'Are you quite finished, Jess?' her English teacher, Mr Price, asked her.

'Yes, sir!' Jess said and sat down.

But everyone else was still laughing.

'Jess, you will never get anywhere in life if you don't apply yourself,' Mr Price said. 'I don't want to hear any of your silly stories ever again!'

Jess shrugged her shoulders. She opened her book.

'Don't worry about him,' her best friend Emma whispered. 'He hasn't got a funny bone in the whole of his body.'

Jess forced a smile. Emma was right. She mustn't let him get her down.

Chapter Two

An evening out

That evening, Jess forgot about Mr Price.

She wrote up her funny story on her blog. A lot of people followed her blog. They often left loads of comments.

Before Jess could finish her blog, the phone rang. It was Emma.

'Do you want to come with me to the comedy club tonight?' Emma asked.

'Wow! That would be great!' Jess said.

Jess finished writing her blog and got ready to go.

She met Emma at the comedy club. Jess was excited.

'There might be an 'open mike' session before the comedians come on,' Jess told Emma. 'That's when anybody can have a go.'

'You could tell some of your stories,' Emma said.

Chapter Three

'He's ruined everything'

Inside the club, Jess noticed someone she knew, sat on the other side of the room.

'Look!' Emma said. 'It's Mr Price.'

'Oh no! I can't do any of my stories now,' Jess said. 'Not after what he said in school this morning.'

Jess was very disappointed.

'Why did Mr Price have to be here?' she moaned. 'He's ruined everything.'

Later in the show, the headline comedian came on stage. She was very funny. The whole audience laughed.

But Jess was not really listening.

'I get most of my jokes from the Internet,' the comedian said. 'One of my favourite blogs is **Jess Terr's Funny Life**. I don't know who Jess Terr is, but she's really funny.'

30

Chapter Four

'Go Jess!'

Jess jumped when she heard her name.

'That's my friend's blog,' Emma shouted out. 'Jess Terr. She's right here!'

Emma pointed at Jess. Jess blushed.

The comedian was amazed to hear that the writer of her favourite blog was in the audience.

'Come up on stage, Jess,' the comedian said.

Emma pushed her out of her seat toward the stage.

'Go Jess!' Emma shouted.

'I think your stories are brilliant,' the comedian said.

'I'm her English teacher,' Mr Price yelled out.

'Jess has a real talent,' the comedian said to Mr Price. 'I hope you support her. One day she could be a great comedy writer.'

Mr Price looked shocked.

'Yes, of course,' he said. 'I always give her all my support.'

Everybody in the audience clapped.

Jess looked at Mr Price.

'Now,' thought Jess, 'things will be different at school.'

Mr Price knew it too.

Curtain Call

audience	laugh
blog	material
career	mime
comedian	miserable
comedy club	open mike
comic	performance
comedian	performer
experience	props
grumpy	risky
headline	session
heckler	sketches
improv	slapstick
joke	theatre